+ LITTLE ENVELOPE OF EARTH CONDITIONS +

+

LITTLE

OF EARTH

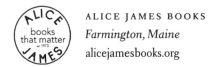

ALICE JAMES BOOKS
Farmington, Maine
alicejamesbooks.org

ENVELOPE

CONDITIONS

+

CORI A.
WINROCK

10 9 8 7 6 5 4 3 2 1

Alice James Books are published by Alice James Poetry Cooperative, Inc.,
an affiliate of the University of Maine at Farmington.

Alice James Books
114 Prescott Street
Farmington, ME 04938
www.alicejamesbooks.org

Library of Congress Cataloging-in-Publication Data

Names: Winrock, Cori A., author.
Title: Little envelope of earth conditions / Cori Winrock.
Description: Farmington, Maine : Alice James Books, 2020
Identifiers: LCCN 2019012544 (print) | LCCN 2019015657 (ebook)
    ISBN 9781948579629 (eBook) | ISBN 9781948579063 (pbk. : alk. paper)
Classification: LCC PS3623.I6637 (ebook) | LCC PS3623.I6637 A6 2020 (print)
    DDC 811/.6—dc23
LC record available at https://lccn.loc.gov/2019012544

Alice James Books gratefully acknowledges support from individual
donors, private foundations, the University of Maine at Farmington, the
National Endowment for the Arts, and the Amazon Literary Partnership.

Cover art: Geneva Library, Arch. de Saussure 66/7, piece 8

CONTENTS

for—

+ my little moonwalkers, Sallie + Rosa

+ my mother, Sally   + the twin

+ *There will come a time when people decide you've had enough of your grief,*
and they'll try to take it away from you. +

—SARAH MANGUSO

+ *and my voice then speaks with*
spaces much as a sewing machine
might write with no thread a line
of small holes +

—ALICE OSWALD

+ *I would look down and say, 'This is the Moon, this is the Moon,' and I would look up*
and say, 'That's the Earth, that's the Earth' +

—ALAN BEAN, APOLLO 12

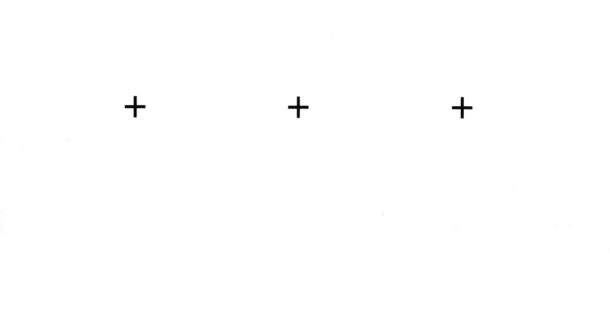

WHAT WOULD HAPPEN TO YOUR BODY IN SPACE WITHOUT A SPACESUIT

+ What you say, you say in a body; you can say nothing
outside of this body +

Whose foreheads should we kiss to check for fever,
whose memories are those we keep

so close to our wrists. The stars are only us
before us, afforded by so much distance.

We have drawn pictures of such animals
we have never seen. We have become such sky

-slung animals in our most untender moments.
Our bodies have been exposed to all sorts of things.

The stars don't believe in weeping us
to sleep or singing us into a new season.

In space we imagine we are holding each other
by the hand instead of holding our own hands

over our mouths. To grieve, to be grieving—
no one is going to come tell us it's not safe

to be holding our breath. We learn to sleep
with our hands in the dark

of strangers' mouths, keep our heads singing
in hopes of bringing our lost

helmets back. How warmblooded
the moon must still seem when seen from the earth.

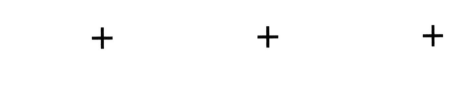

A DAUGHTER DRAFTS A LETTER FROM EARTH: DEPARTURE

Dear _____,

What repair. What weather system permitting
mourning, some music, the hollowbody
dress of a loved one. What worry I do nothing

humbly—dream the branches of your blood
lines as sunprint—. Feel creased as—.
What touch I've nailed to me I've nailed to me
instead of all these cliff swallows. Their mud nests

suffocating the eaves. What refusal
to see ourselves to sleep until we rinse
our feet—. Until someone has tied red threads
around my ankle to ward off a new year. In the field-dark

the storm hovers, the cows sound
a riled sadness. What heat
lightning rising. Reverberant sky.

I am radioing from myself
to myself. Endless desert
where I thought a drop-dead
winter should be. Some nights this

is all I can do to keep from—. I drink myself into a threat
to sleep off my dress
by morning. What static electricity when we're still

in the eye of it. Thunder slow-dilating

                  overhead like a train whistle. The lake swallowing

      the thrill of lightning lines.

              My only desire a desire to touch

           —no one—for a year. Let the storm drag me

bodyless into the hush of long grasses,

             fields brushed with sage, wait for someone

        more remorseful—to pass through. —I'm leaving

with the perfume rising off my hair, two children

        asleep in their nests.

LOVE POEM IN A TIME OF AMBULANCES

The moon scrapes her face across the body

         of the ambulance idling below—O little empire

of emergency, O altar of resuscitation: I kneel down in you

           like I kneel my grief down in the dive bar—throat haloed

    in administered kisses, mouth full of salt.

         Or this is a grief that refuses to arouse

even a candle

         of a name. So I do not offer one. I genuflect with the light.

And so what of the lawlessness

         of these rescuers in white—wild west their tendencies of mercy

then none. Pistols blazing to observe who draws first.

         Then the single bullet straight through my surrender-

raised hand. See how even the smallest hole still smokes.

           I bring the mob that knows to light the monster

on fire & we do: the ambulance keening, the ambulance as ablaze as the virgin

         mary's heart. And so what if these are my marys

burning? Or that I meant to say

         my mothers. My mother's body disbursed

in flame. How a body is burned until gathered,

    until it remains—. And O to be the curve of the ambulance's bones,

         its frame picked to glittering

         in the parking lot. The birds now recircling—a moment blown

backward as if from a blast of electromagnetic waves. I strip

    off our hospital gown and release it

         out an open window. The ash ascends as a humiliation

of sparrows. I lay myself down in the afterflash

of the ambulance's light. Wait for my temperature to rise.
For you to come press your wrist against my wrist

                                    to see if my pulse is still
tucked inside. Over and over the ambulance shudders

                              like a shocked heart, revives.

LANDSCAPE IN WHICH I AM OBLITERATED BY LIGHT

+ innocent sleep, sleep that knits up the ravell'd sleave of care +

Nothing fits properly in this space, Little Sleeve.
Are you watching? The way I am crawling across

the walls of every room of the house like a wet
near-dead thing. Like the sad sack that I am.

Little sleeve, the dead are everywhere
in my poems & I've forgotten the living

body is a necessary antecedent
to landscape. Landscape of unfreezing cells,

of new ringing forests; landscape of remorseless
heat & dry light. Little sleeve, spring is coming

coming & dragging its thaw & snow-shedding
stink. Little sleeve, the yard is dismantling its panoptic

mantling of white. & I want to be sucked into
the mud's black hole vacuum instead of mapping

our way to another doctor. I swear I once heard someone
say there are only so many images a body can take

before the skeleton is stolen in light. Is it a given
that every TV emergency ends

in joyous resuscitation? Little sleeve, I left
my teenage bones to winter

as X-rays in a folder in a drawer.
There is a run in the quietness

of every pair of my stockings.
Little sleeve, so many bodies are denied

as bodies. & your body is not even.
We are animals, are being resurrected from DNA,

& the youngest ever brain frozen for a new body
to be built for her 500 years into a future.

Little sleeve, Is this really what we call saving?
Across an ocean drones are banqueting

as bees as bombs in bridal arrangements
& we call this progress. The satellites are monitoring

our devolving. Little sleeve, How does love appear
in no gravity? Like love, like love.

Little sleeve, no one has told me what happens
when I reemerge to a thawing

earth. What happens when a daughter returns
from the underworld to the exact moment. The exact

same grove of known trees. But no mother. No child.
Little sleeve-of-her-own-accord. Little ravel:

I've dug up the bulb of our girlhood
body from the frozen yard as if everything stays

perennial. As if aster rather than ash. I've buried
our hands in my mouth. Little sleeve, always

on the cusp of these two bright emergency
rooms, Demeter's gorgeous force

on the brink. Come & get me, I'd like to hear myself
say: to be contagious: to be uncontained.

Little sleeve, you are distilled to a certificate
we signed before we could leave the hospital

with your sister. Little little, sing
to me. Little little, sleeve me

tender. My throat is worn slender
as a seam, my heart gone to seed.

Little, it's impossible to turn around
to tell if what is spilling from us is water or salt

or star. Little sleeve, your legs are dragging behind me.
I swear nothing will fit in this spacesuit but us.

RÉSEAU PLATE: INTERIOR WITH GEMINI CONSTELLATION

Call it a piano tucked inside a houseboat. The woods that turn us
inside out: heart which is not a salt lick. Deer which will no longer
graze at our wrists at sundown. Our hands are open because they are
empty. We've cuffed ourselves tight at the wrists with what is
left of daylight. We've cuffed ourselves to the snow. The landscape:
a hospital. The heartache: a cliché. They say what heals is to saw
one's self in half & walk away as miracle. When I found out I was
harboring an asterism of hearts, no one starred the sick one's closed.
No one kissed us congratulations. Inside you pressed yourselves together
like two playing cards, faces in profile. We embroidered your hands
as an offering. We measured the distance in pulses. The variable light
of your leftover X-rays still slices us off at the wrist. Your sister develops
in the open air as if dipped in chemicals in a dark room. When the house
-lights come on like an ambulance's dazzle, we've already left our bodies
to science, we've let the unbearable constellation be halved.

BUZZ ALDRIN'S FIRST WORDS ON THE MOON AS ELEGY

Salt Lake City, Utah

The mountains wallpaper the city in snow, in not-another-
              word: O faceted animals in whiteshift, what *beautiful,*

       beautiful is this? *Magnificent desolation.* Our bodies pinned
                     open into the last kind blues

       of NyQuil. I have nothing to say
about what the moon is doing

              now, (*beautiful. view*), or to this unendingly ghostless
                     house. Or to you, who have taken

to re-creating our expected life
              in diminuendos—tiny us

       with newborns, tiny us with so little
                     light—for shame for shame.

What is grief but a syllable that accumulates
              us of our gravity. Love, the moon is cutting

       its teeth on our bedroom floor.
                     How underwhelming its apprehensive

              face, how glozing. *Contact. Magnificent.* We've been sleeping
on top of the covers like dollhouse

lovers. And love, love I've unstuck every glow-
        in-the-dark star left tacked to the ceiling—

as if we might be allowed to circle back to the before
        of each other. To reappear in the salt

lake and to know the right meaning—.
        What we buried we think we have buried

        for good. *Magnificent. Shutdown.* Then spring.
Then thaw that strips our voices back to us

        as static: *contact light. Beautiful engine.*
            We bury each other

this way because *desolation, view* it is the way we would like
        to be buried.

        We tell ourselves it's a fever. A season. *Magnificent* the mountains
            still doing their heavy confections. *Desolation.*

        We bury each other this way *beautiful, beautiful*
            because it is the way we would like to be buried.

On the lake's edge: the abandoned bodies
        of our spacesuits. I climb inside yours. I wake it. I wake it.

MICROCHIMERA AS LULLABY

Shush, littlest bones, still in your first ring
of growth—the skeleton, singing
its diminutives: good night nobody
good night mush. It's tone-dark in the body
of the woods—the map marked with Xs
that multiply & hide—genetics' convex
revision: all night you've been sleepcrawling
through the walls—pitching, yawing. Darling,
don't say a word—I've rubbed our ghosts
raw as the floorboards, grafted us—almost.
The sonographer's Doppler: a canary—
the bloodhush warbling its own obituary.
I dream your buried X-rays as errata—& you:
a bur in my cells: a fermata.

EULOGY

I carried one grief while courting
another—

Because the moon pulled in
a tide of early dirt—

Because I could not bury both
my mother and a child

Because the living
child wanted to go to that place, mama—

With the beautiful stones, where people leave
flowers and presents

And now we are up each night with her sleepless
fear of falling

into those dark holes.

Because the dirt was too—
And my hands were—.

I'm throwing red thread over my shoulders,
salting my grievances.

Listen, in the woods
we are banished from—

the owls are giving back the bones
of the ones—if they lived

we might have loved.

HOW TO PUT ON A SPACESUIT

+ If I speak for the dead, I must leave +

The neighborhood shimmies on out

Of its streetlights. Surrounding our mouths

Each night, the overblown peony

Clouds of the bereaved—our daughters asleep

In their bodies, dreaming their woodsman

-less woods. The mice sleepcrawling

Through the walls. I enter the airlock—: the trees bare

Or about-to. A wrist mirror and checklist

On my sleeves: *I was running, I ran, I will be—.*

I veil my face to keep from beginning

To pre-breathe, to forgo the endless necessity

For nitrogen—our lady of gravity:

For you—I put on my one, white

Dress and wait for the bees

To fall far from the tree.

WHEN HER HANDS ARE STOLEN THROUGH A LEFT-OPEN WINDOW

When you were young the birds came at night to eaves
        -drop your words—the birds with their beaks open

    as psalms—your hands wrapped in a telephone cord,
your mouth the mouth of a fever.

      The birds learned the language you passed back
         & forth between yourself & another, other-tongue of tendering

        —of small towns & sod lawns, of motorcycle billboards
  & so, so many siblings. Not yet my language of remorse

& desert heat. Not yet the words of grief / of binds / of knives & eye
        -hooks we learn to swallow. The birds came to your childhood

    house & they listened like broaches pinned to the eaves.
        & then you were grown. & then you were married & then

    came babies in two bright carriages. & then you were
singing & stitching & undone. & then you were tired & merry

        & blue, blue as your anti-static smock, as the circuits
you fused. And then you—*The woman in the ambulance / Whose red heart blooms*

   through her coat so astoundingly. And the birds arrived on the eve
        of—. & they opened, were humming. Yes the birds blown

through the window an omen, a homing, a carrier
of grief—yes the birds flown through the house

meant someone soon would be dying. Yes I closed
your hospital window & the ambulance carried me

forward to my childhood, yes I blew the candles
to light & opened the windows of my room—

and the birds came forth they came forth & parroted you back
to me as static. Yes, these birds that stole your words

through the left-open window—these birds which carried
the voice of your voice to the future, which telegraphed

its sadness, which signaled to others that these were
words of the person I might name my mother.

Yes I willed them to grieve your words & myself to hold them
still until they were no longer able.

DILORICATION⁺ BEGINS AT THE SILK OF A WRIST

+ to rip open a sewn piece of clothing

For you I refused to sit still under the draped lead, to put on the dissolvable
blue paper dress, to allow myself to be exposed down

to the permanent specter of the X-rayed.
I let my shadows rend straight from grey to cavity. Saved all my static

electricity for nearly a year just to cup your resurrected hands. Your resurrected hands
that fit, so ungloved, so willing between the fulcrum of my grieving

jaw & my too-narrow shoulder. Don't call me rhododendron,
your little epaulette. I recognize our body as a confusion

of flowers or hands. My proscenium, my floweret. What I want
is so simple, so simple as to defibrillate what we may have

already forgotten: our temporarily collective skeleton. The stranger
in the grocery store, in a sally-red wool coat, that I bargained to recollect me

as daughter. My grandest ambition: an unrippable second dress.
And for you, my floating bones, my fledgling, not to become

the mother who dissolves in someone's slow-receding window—
the man I watched from the driver's seat of my winter-hot

-housed car, resuscitated again & again in the dazzle
of an ambulance. His clothes surely ripped quick

at the initial scene, stripped first from wrist to shoulder for the bee-sting
swell of a needle & threaded line. His wedding ring already being passed

from daughter to daughter's daughter to unknown
                     unwed hand. I take back what I said

          about the dress. I take the part about unbecoming
back & bury it, every year, with your namesake. Leave my wrists

               between sleeve & glove bare: winter
                   the cuff of exposed skin. I kneel down as if prayer

          inside your photograph, your sloughed-off communion
glove. Crawl along the near-dissolved cup of its palm, lay myself down

in each of the five slender hallways—little isolettes:
                 won't you cure me. Won't you tell me whose wrist will test the heat

     of my forehead, check me for fever when the dove of her hands
                      are stolen through a left-open window.

+ WENT WEEPING, LITTLE BONES. BUT WHERE? +

Inside the dark you grow like a horror
film—limbless fish

without eyes. Today your skeleton begins
its marrowing somewhere: balled up

as an owl pellet. In the apartment
we're lecherous in the damp of hot-

water heaters—the sheets kicked off
as of November for good; the sex a tender

hooking. Even after, my lover & I keep leaving
swelter-rings of teeth marks on each other's

thighs from frustration. From bed, the treeline:
endless crows the city harasses to eradicate

with light & amplified sirens. We find them,
one by one, dead in the parking lots

downtown. Their stiff-lozenge bodies &
polite-crossed legs. Something I could learn

from—how to be happening but not
sad tableau. As far off as prediction—

your augury heart settled in its nest.
What are the blood results of all this

foretelling? What do I do with what I might have
wanted? My center of gravity

already tipped. Even now I'll insist we put our hands
on the pulse to know it's actually ours.

SUCH & SUCH HAPPENS & I HEAR MUSIC

boxes being sprung. And what could I say—
I found you, furled in the hothouse of a hospital gown

little red ridings still unfledged inside
the wolf. Not yet teething your way through

the hyper-floraled mess of spring, not yet a season
where other children's bones turn over

faster in the garland-dark. How do I tell
the bees I know: time ruins the honey

ruins the hive: a barter is a daughter *or*
her mother's mother allowed to stay

alive. Let me be teeming-with, caught
with feathers in my mouth. On the brink of cradling

my own neck between my teeth.
Instead you hand me two envelopes,

two omens: when the grievers open
their beaks, when all my eyes and

hooks have come unclosed. Even the woodsmen
with their stethoscopes pressing the leaves:

like dresses, like X-rays: cannot summon the dead
-sound of no bleating, its blank

repeating song. Your newborn hands wolving
for heat inside the hive.

+ ALL BY MYSELF I AM A HUGE CAMELLIA +

Some days no one is my mother
but my mother. & my mother is no

longer a distance that cinches itself—
the flush on flush of the new

fever, the baby's first floral-
heat nursed down—with a telephone

call. I could not gather, could not
collect your voice in fits

in tinder in sleep. So the flowerbeds:
empty. The endless ringing: all hesitation,

no digging. I wake to bury
you again, stumbling

for the rotary receiver on its vine—
swinging from the wall of a house

I left burning-small: votive
light throwing off no sound.

In the yard the petals all flame
& lantern. In the crib

my daughter moro-s herself
in heartbeat cycles, limbs sparked

apart with shock. The smoke of us both
rises: like a moon: like a pulse. & I am

alone in our surveillance, our time-
lapsed fevering burst into a single bloom

: the resurrected echo-light of your ambulance
dissolving through the walls.

LAW OF DIMINISHING RETURNS

for Nicci

In a copse the deer's body is glass
-felled, is still-beating
cross sections, is abrupt-

bladed. The deer's body
is my body. And we are not
waiting for each other

in some teenage kind of way.
What I wish I were saying:
Eurydice follows her mother

instead of her lover. I am tired
of glances as apologia.
My ribcage & trussings are heavy

-hemmed with sludging
through snow: two white deer
that were not ghosts. When we saw them

—in the army depot in upstate,
against an apocalyptic sunset: splitting
a landscape into two perfect halves

of light and no light—they were real.
And I am halved again. My sudden sight.
My mouth open-enough to sing

into. Don't tell me she slipped
away or between—. That the doe I am
has already been sliced.

A slip is a minor mistake, a made-
haste, as in: *Her gorgeous slip*
of the tongue spoiled

the surprise. A tongue
does not always want
its wanting. I love you I love.

I know you. I know you
will not return or the same.
Even if I promise I'm floored

by all this horizonline, this butterflying
of animalbody on roadsides,
the trees keep glistering us

into a distance. I want to yell at all the dead
deer to just get the fuck up
until they do. I lullaby the seasons.

WISTERIA SNARES THE NEAREST BODY

Hours after disembarking, a body might still believe it is
on the boat: a ferry and its circular windows like a mourning

ring strung on a neck. Or the loop of hair we did not snip
in your hospital rooms. It felt like a wash cycle when we slept

on the waves—the boat growing around our glass
O like a meant-to-say-sorry. A carousel of sicknesses

buffed to their brights. Though no apology for how
we carried your cell wreckage off as ash

in our hands, forgot how to allow, let alone
let go on loop. I wished for the heaviest

brass diving bell my head could carry, to be asked to shore
up a cathedral from six meters deep.

Instead every morning I discover your head
on our front lawn being pilfered by birds.

Then your hands and feet.
What do you call the remorse of leaving someone

on accident again? To be compulsive enough to tattoo your radiation
constellation across my chest as if heirloom?

If I rescue your bed from a sinking
ICU—. Float it to the forest encircled in life

preservers—. Drag it by teeth in a fit—. I won't tell you
sleeping inside the forest means separating

your legs from your body as if for safe
-keeping. The birds in focus in the foreground. Birds as holes

in the wisteria wallpaper. The birds that tear our agency
off as a tender loophole.

+   +   +

HOW TO SEW A SPACESUIT, 1968

Dear _____,

I've taken to pinning patterns on your bedroom floor
$\qquad\qquad$ where we dragged the sweating moon.
$\qquad$ Practical astronomy—our seam allowances
smaller than a sewing needle's eye. Above us, the ceiling strewn with flowers
$\qquad$ cut from the leftover wallpaper of another room.
$\qquad\qquad$ If you can't dampen your grief,
$\qquad\qquad\qquad$ what will keep your fingers from being lured
$\qquad\qquad$ under the needle in sleep, from the bared teeth
$\qquad\qquad\qquad$ of the feed dog gathering up fabric in the wake
$\qquad$ of our hands? Remember—one stitch fired
$\qquad\qquad\qquad$ per footfall means fewer discarded suits.
$\qquad\qquad$ If you can't forgive your scissors—chalk this constellation overhead: the long arm
of the machine where we turn & turn again the whole body of your future
$\qquad\qquad$ daughter's spacesuit.
$\qquad\qquad\qquad$ About heirlooms, you know what they say— + *We will have to split one*
$\qquad\qquad\qquad$ *needle / this winter—one end for me, / one end for air.* +

$\qquad\qquad\qquad$ How we make do and mend is not always fair.

DÉBRIDEMENT

When I find out I'm pregnant I bury my wedding dress
in the front yard—letting everyone in the neighborhood watch me

peel the blue satin over my head: my slipless figure & a shovel.
The school bus slowing its yellow dredge to witness the anxiety

of the uncovered. I dig a tunnel to my grandmother straight through
my mother—her old flower bulbs empty rattles, their bodies now fists

in earth. I lick my ungloved hands & gather fragments of bone & leftover
teeth into my mouth. How else to feed the matryoshkaed body, its double

hummingbird hearts? Ashes. Ashes. In the tunnel I uncover a nightgown
I sloughed off as I lost my virginity to a song about elevens; crawl back into

its florals & incorporeal sense of expectation—the assistant's glittering self
sawed open to applause. Down here my new cluster of cells can't echo or mirror.

It lullabies me with replication. Tells me to revisit the rooms I flooded
just to peel off the wallpaper, to uproot the ugly azaleas from the family

before & before. When I arrive at my childhood I undress
the house like a wound.

THE WAY WE SLEEP

+ I confuse everything for myself +

The towns inside me are small as hand mirrors—the holiday lights still up at Easter.
Though no one is sodding the backyards for precision anymore & I am no virgin
in waiting. Lately in the hatbox I keep the heat that followed your ambulance
to its snowed-in hospital lot. A curve I can only unmap by deribboning
the cassette tapes I played until stripped, one by one. Everywhere the heart a condition of
folding & arrangement of parts. In the saloned photographs my mother's beautiful
teenage hands around a rotary telephone. & I am learning that mourning is neither doorway nor
switchboard. I am trying to complicate the disordered geometry of loss: as in, locate the pink
walls behind her. In unmade home movies I take the back stairwell of her childhood
house down to the side door—the walls papered in a billboard motorcycle ad, the pixels
so exposed they are just static. I try to align myself only with angles & forced perspective:
flowers, necklines, cones, my breasts in a bra. An unzipped dress's precise corner: the clothed
& unclothed body meeting like mirrors, cheating the eye to see a more open space.
Yes I have heard the story of a boy that ran past the cliff edge, the riverbank catching him
broken. My grandmother, who sent everyone to play away from the fresh-laid lawns,
as aflame with guilt as the Virgin Mary's heart: every house within me kept hot by this
grief. Know that I have driven the same Main Street route for every funeral ever attended—
a telephone cord wrapped around my hand until circulation is lost. Inside, my towns reflect
such N-scale scenes: every season Christmas again, the lift bridges strangled
with tinseled ice & headlights. On the highway out I mistake the rush of the dead
leaves for birds erupting in a tight net. & I close my eyes as if waiting for a second
or third kiss, press my thighs into the callused burnmarks in the upholstery until I am the fever
-seeking body before the rush of air before the ash.

OSTENTATIOUS STILL LIFE WITH HOSPITAL & BODY OF

I won't start your ghost on the shore. I won't even stand near
the water with flowers in my hands.

Carrying your body over the ocean has kept it
ossuary for years. And every day needs a thousand gilt cells

between having to choose: you as landscape or you as the bray
of a fever of ambulances.

Through the walls their parade
lanterns like snow-notes, like I conjure you—

+

But what sorry ambulances that merely appear to be
moving. The old rolling car effect. I know,

    I know. And when you left—No ghost.

And what sorry landscape without
ghost. Without empire. Without sorry

moon. Like what are we desirous of if not ghosting.
If not old acquaintances of another drab New Year

    la fin-ing the party in tinsel and no stockings.

+

No paper chain of holiday girls holding hands. Because no

holding hands. No folded readouts. No something
        borrowed, something new.

                +

For better light I had to rearrange
                myself (and you) on the table waiting

to be a study-of. Bodying but no longer
                        sallying forth.

                +

I wanted to speak to myself as a form
                of capture. What I am saying is the mirror,

is abeyance. I'm asking for a solution that doesn't
                involve lavishing you in, strapping you

to the landscape, taking no ghost
                for an answer.

X-RAY PASTORAL

+ In space—on nights when there was no moon, it was difficult for me to tell
the Earth from the sky— +

Sent for everything capsuled in a blankness. A leeching of—.
My hands cupping nothing and utterly unasked for.

It is whiting-out here, a hospitaled sky.
Every grass-blade lapsed into the almost opaque

state of scotch tape (the flimse & gauze of lingerie held
up against the light). A shortwave, a landscape draped

to leaden. From out here I listen, like a nurse, to the induced
paper-whites burst like heartbeats on chilled countertops.

Nothing swathes, or fogs. The marrow undarking
around this small field of our grief.

Look how the bleached horizons lay down like cirrusbone-
clouds across the lake. Look how the dendritic

branches exact themselves into a mirror, haul up
their roots to suck on the sky. Love, let us be rid of

the abrasion of vividness. The bright bulk
of dandelions, mums, the clot of forget-me-nots.

Let us perform an aftermath in blue—our marriage stop-
bathed at the almost-see-through.

When they trace our negatives under florescent lamps,
they won't see the perfect white corners of our house

like surgery sheets—coruscant, tucked in tight.
A deconstructed wedding dress crushed into the cedar chest.

SPACESUIT IN EARLY DECEMBER WOODS

+ Because I know you not as a lover loves, I know it was me who replaced

your backless gown—let myself let myself see: body—undressed you into

this white, work-a-day suit. + I remember there was no sense of rush.

I was embroidering your initials as tight stitches in the cuffs: red threads

to net you to these woods, to particulars, to this cove of known trees. I called out

the family names for each of us, whittled a heart into the burls: reckoned

future distances in precision-planed knots and cross sections. + Even as I kept

forgetting every thing, I knew it was not me that left + your feet dangling,

embedded in wet leaves—in this not-thaw because before-frost.

Your face was tipped away, already. + I remember I held that: my inherited

hand near the hospital bed's edge. Wrung the sleeves soaked in mud. Again.

+ How many times? Each time I stumble into this moment I try to stay

inaudible like I don't want to wake you, but this isn't sleeping. I won't wake

any moment either. + You are simply that—I found this clearing. I dressed you.

I did not dress you as when-fall-gets-winter. Instead I prepared the almost snow for the terrible humming of spring, then summer. + Gave it your frame.

Let the trees grow their years in rings. +

+

The griever awaits in a room with a horse-

drawn ambulance idling in her chest—
her dowry an empire of snowed-over

backstreets. No sidewalks salted; no plows
dredging their residual black asphalt

demilunes. The sawing sound comes
from above not below—it's the moon drawing

a tune from a bow's warp & halving, the grief's

wet dress & the grief: eyelets & yes-
lets, exposed neck & hands: post flammable.

The ambulance a tindering stalled. A cure-all.

Inside the plastic bags of funeral flowers the cut
stems exhale the walls to condensation, like too-much

kissing in a fastened car: a breathpattern:
the fingerdrawn heart & its banal arrow-

pierce. But I am forgetting to pronounce
the grief still aflame—the yahrzeit undoused

inside her half-open mouth. I am forgetting
to define that I'm still the griever—

the shock always a palpable suitor;
my own little defibrillator.

AUBADE FOR FUTURE RESURRECTION

I arborglyph our initials into the trees and the little white dress
      in my heart says *bang bang*, lays herself down

like a crime scene. I imagine this is how it feels
when the small church of birds in your hands

refuses to lift its hem of song. Never mind the pins
and needles attending my body as if

felled. Never mind the aspen-psalms, the burls, their zillion unblinking
      eyes. Your perfume brays off until I am sugar

-less under the sheer force of unfloral light—
light so pre-winter low it splits

the wood to shadow. Splits the wood
      back to salt. Even for those of us who kept such vigil-

moons: no arrival, no avowal. The forest refuses to laurel
its leaves around our chalk outlines. And I'm not drunk

enough to admit this must feel like when God stops
      talking to even the most devoured in faith.

Love, let me pin me open before you
begin the autopsy: our morningfog

voices coming through my coat

    as so many hand-embroidered ambulances.

THE YEAR WE DID NOT PULL OUR BODIES FROM THE LAKE

How sorry the laundromat's light-flood, its reiterated tableau:
    round windows like space helmets opening onto our touching
        clothes. The salt rings that make it clear we've been touching, together
    underwater. How sorry the honey I refused, the falter.
And now you pulling someone's warm spacesuit from the washing machines. Tell me again
        how no one's stories are redeeming us—. How I'm driving across
            state lines to rewrite the interior: the desire for you
    to undress my body from the lake. This is the version
where all of the wives are killed. And I can no longer tell
        the difference between U-Haul & ambulance,
      beekeeper & astronaut. The ending which feels like being carried
    from the hive, the ending which is us not undressing ourselves
          of the empty room: its spare filament. I want you to tell me
    again how we are convinced of taking
          a stranger's still-wet clothes
with the intention of tenderness toward each other—
      that next time we might pull ourselves clean
            as an incision from the lake.

+ A REAL SPACESUIT IS A LITTLE ENVELOPE OF EARTH CONDITIONS +

—*Douglas Lantry*

+

When our mothers were astronauts, we sewed space

-suits from donated wedding dresses

so we could buy better thread. We sewed day into night

for the moonwalkers, gathering bolts of

constellation in our arms. After every performance

we waited behind stage—taking measurements, giving

compliments. They loved us.

It was spring. We were sewing, the astronauts

were singing, and inside our body

53

+

two babies were turning.
They loved us so—so we sewed & sewed
when we were the daughter for the astronauts—we waltzed
onstage singing: *in my moon suit and funeral veil I am*
no source of honey. So why should they turn on me? Tomorrow
I will be sweet—. The bees were sewing air,
we were bowing—gathering the meadow
thrown around us. Inside us: twin moon faces
reflecting in profile.

+

If the astronauts were our daughters—
if they were ours, were ours—they inherited
their spacesuits from our abandoned
trousseaus, gathering around them
in meadows. They took in old seams. Repaired our stitched
réseaus—marking & measuring & singing back
-stage: *There is a needle fair Though no appearance indicate –'Tis threaded
in the Air –*. Inside each bridal chest—
two envelopes waiting to be turned

+

into wedding dresses. It was spring.

There was applause.

Then the astronauts left. Then our dead mothers left.
The spacesuits were abandoned
on the theater floor. The bees left. The singing left.

Then we stayed.
Didn't we? Didn't we let ourselves X-ray
each other. Didn't we kneel down to listen
inside the spacesuits. Didn't we pre-breathe. Inside—a constellation
in half. Inside the envelopes only one

+

baby was teething. We stitched the empty envelope

closed. We dug a hole in the stage & placed the body of our baby

girl in the box from the sewing machine.

We wanted a larger cemetery.   We let the hospital's

opera have the box. I did everything

ourselves. I even managed to put on the moon

-suit somehow. I even managed to—yes, I sang: *Fetch the seam I missed –*

Closer – so I – at my sleeping –

Still surmise I stitch –. I turned my face to the dark

+

opera house—: on stage I was mewling, the astronauts were no longer
returning, and inside my body no babies
were singing. You did not love me. It was spring.
After the performance I hid
behind stage—mistaking sureness, grieving
compliance. I had sung & I had sewed—
night gathering the constellation that was left
in my arms. She and I had missed our entrance, so I sewed isolette
dresses from deconstructed spacesuits,
so I could bury the dead.

+

As I unthreaded we sang we sang: *But not the Grief – that*
nestled Close
As Needles –

+

We were so close. We bundled up the envelopes.

A DAUGHTER SENDS THE STENOGRAPHER A LAST LETTER
FROM THE MOON

Dear -S [record: *dear Sir / desire / Sally*] —

In spite of myself I   *Pronounce each word aloud ; be sure*

Up here there's nothing   to hear. What does it mean

that everything you recorded was said

by another. Dear   *To write just* what you hear—*no more :*

Mama—Where I write to you now are we remaining

in a version in which there are a grove of ambulances

All silent letters please ignore.

or ambivalences. Mama,   tonight I walk off

my ambulances in someone else's cemetery—

Leave out the E in PANE

headstones which belong

to other grievers. Tonight it's snowing and snowing again.
The deer bent low in the body

The L—not heard—in CHALK or PALM;

of ambulances. The deer turning
toward us, pin-still in ambivalence. Or can I no longer tell

the difference between deer

The H in HEIR, the B in DOUBT

and headstones in this weather—laying themselves down in rings
of thawed-out grass. Mama, the salt lake has been filling

never sounded—leave them out.

with snow—I'm flying
low over this ridiculous landscape. Returning

the P and L in PSALM;

from orbit to another new house. Or the lake
is filling with ambulances and this sorry moon and I'm in love with another

life—one where you are

soft, an S—as FACT or FACE;

still or gone and I'm considering taking

a lover. I keep trying to write a poem without

C-H in ACHE is simply

desire—   without this sorry

moon. Your name a shorthand   a lullaby back down to ground

-control a sound I gave   a daughter

C is like S in ICE or CEASE

another record   *And this each single sound express*

of grief   of what is left.

By what you hear—*no more, no less.*

PETRICHOR

+ What lingers + in the airlock + after + what's trapped + in the folds + of the spacesuit + like ozone + like welding fumes + charred sparklers + the universe + starting stars + breaking +   down   +   this overheating   + engine + wet clothing after + rolling around + in snow + the entryway + to this childhood + house + thrown off + like a second + less suitable + body +

A DAUGHTER REVISES A LETTER FROM EARTH: RE-ENTRY

+ Had my first backwards dream last night—

got back to Earth and gravity wasn't normal +

You only have to be on the ground for a week before the dreams begin to return
you—pulled toward the center of the earth

just like everyone, you are pulled toward the dirt. If you look directly

+

at the dead in a dream, they vanish—tether them in your peripheral vision, in the daily

before it takes your breath. The cliff swallows
in their mud nests, still suffocating the eaves.

+

And here is the scene deprived of gravity—the mosquitos hitching a ride in the galaxy
of my hair: their whine coming alive

in the quiet inside the house. The careful way one unwraps
a bar of soap in a clean hotel room: it floats off

like a note—little undone envelope.

+

And the shrew eating insects in the windowsill—small as a finger

-print, I'll leave in the freezer so we can study it.

+

They say *such love* in small burials—wrapped in two jackets, tucked in

a tea box. But I did not inter her. I turned my back

to the dirt—I looked up, I unearthed

her—.

+

They say all we needed to do to blot out the moon

was place a hand over her

it-will-all-be-fine face, shut one eye each.

+

Listen, listen—

every time I've tried to bring our baby back

to the ground in our old city, I keep burning off all her heat.

HOW TO REMOVE A SPACESUIT

Let go of the furious blur of the monotonous
                    arrival of an emergency—the quaintness

                                   of a cake's circular glow.
                    Our hospital gowns ghosting, inaudible
                                   in the washing machine. Then stop.

             Let go the snowsuit carried
across the parking lot, its accumulation of prints.
             The X-rays of ourselves in stop-motion

                    sequence: my mama's hands, wished-on and just blown
             out. Then stop. Someone else's blood has been diffused

                    into my blood. So let go the deer,
                           the deer that keep arriving, broken-

necked on the highway shoulder. Then stop. The door opening to yellow
                           leaves confettied across the floor.

Let go the ambulance and its after-
             burn: the inconsolable empire of red-flowering
                           notes. They are not coming for us—

      so stop. But love, love don't—
                    stop, I will tell you again—how to let this light go out

from under us. Let the body. Let it—.
Other hearts resume their gravity. Or stop.

I subtract myself from one
spacesuit, then another: those sleeping does.
Pull myself up by my own hair.

Let each wick be lit
with the heat from the last. I'll gather my daughters

around the ordinary
like a birthday.

STILL LIFE IN RÉSEAU PLATE

Like Victoriana mansions in emptying fields + like this room is a body left to light

its way through a house + left to spoil + the wallpaper developing us

as stop-motion + as clattering through space + not stars so much as dark-

stockings-dark + or how to drape our lack + reflection +

above the mirror + the moon is not + for disappearing + above the mirror +

the corners of an unzipped dress + swallowed by the swallowed

overlap of light + the shutter biting down + on its own open hand +

a moment gloved + on film + unto heirloom + the sound of a heavy dress +

dragging + particular + so particular + we are continuous + & appearing + not at all

like a mirror + see-through & astoundingly + not at all

unhusked + as body + as lightseep + as grief + as the house left to dark

+ in its constricted frame.

POLAROID ODE

O four cornered room
in which we tuck the ever-
developing light of our warm
bodies. O snapshot, O ether
-ized flash of childhood—swarm
of chemicals murmuring together
to form empty sky, exposing
day's blue dissolve from blue.
O bad 70's plaid sofas
& pearl snapshirts, costumes
fading like Fisher-Price cars
on washed out lawns. O moon
boots without stars.
O family re-gathering as light-
seep, as grief. O ablation
& emulsion & actual moon—
you day-lurker, you—
balloon I imagine deflating
above our duplex—why the resistance?
Tell me who was in our living room
to capture this instant, whose hand
was shaking us into existence.

HOW TO PRESERVE A SPACESUIT

+ *Never try to move the suit alone—always involve at least two people.* +

+

The birds are whistling better stitches

+

into the wind—fastening us

+

to the meadow, to the edge of

+

the lake where we kneel

+

to fill each spacesuit

+

with flowers then light

+

them on fire. Send their bodies off

+

into the water—   I want the dead to say things

+

I want the dead to say things

+

as they are—a singular motion

+

of an axe to split the wood in half.

+

To sting, to extinguish—

+

it's more like a wet leaf pressed

+

to the chest, cold

+

stethoscope. The heartbeat turned

+

inside out. On the shore: always the ones

+

whose grief is a train

+

whistle reiterating overhead.

+

In the lake, always the dead

+   +

saying: quarantine   the inconsolable.

+

Slow burn rising

+   no moon

+

until we uproot the birds'

+

errant stitches, snip sung threads

+

so we can sleep

+

with their song

+

in our own dry beds.

+

Then daylight.   +   New suture.

+

Then our spacesuits surfacing,   +

washing up

+

again, whole

+

again in the lake's cold skin. I reach down

+

to lift our helmets

+

full of the wind which keeps us

+

warm—I put my mouth to our wrist-

+

mirrors and the light does its slow-graze.

+

I compress our chests,

+

turn our bodies to flood

+

the flowers back

+

into the meadow. On our knees again

+

we uproot this garment

+

again little ache again this time we take it

+

apart, this time   +

                  again we begin

            +

            to make do, to mend.

ATTRIBUTION OF QUOTES

What Would Happen to Your Body in Space: from Wittgenstein

Landscape in which I am Obliterated by Light: from Shakespeare's *Macbeth*

Buzz Aldrin's First Words: from NASA transcripts

How to Put on a Spacesuit: from "Author's Prayer," Ilya Kaminsky

When Her Hands Are Stolen: from "Poppies in October," Sylvia Plath

Went Weeping, Little Bones: from "I Cry, Love! Love!" Theodore Roethke

All By Myself I am a Huge Camellia: from "Fever 103°," Sylvia Plath

How To Sew a Spacesuit: from "Living it Up," Max Ritvo

The Way We Sleep: from Francesca Woodman

X-Ray Pastoral: from "Single Room, Earth View," Sally Ride, *Smithsonian Air & Space Magazine*, 2012

Aubade for Future Resurrection: with a mondegreen from Kevin Prufer

A Real Spacesuit is a Little Envelope: written in dialog with Ilya Kaminsky's "Little Pot"

   title from "Dress for Egress: The Smithsonian National Air and Space Museum's Apollo Spacesuit Collection," Douglas Lantry, *Journal of Design History*, 2001

italicized lines from "Arrival of the Bee Box," Sylvia Plath and [F1468] [F421] & [F681], Emily Dickinson

Petrichor: from *What's It Like in Space: Stories from Astronauts Who've Been There*, Ariel Waldman

A Daughter Revises a Letter from Earth: Re-Entry: Reid Wiseman, tweet from the International Space Station

A Daughter Sends the Stenographer a Last Letter: from "Pitman's Shorthand Rhymes : Writing by Sound"

How to Preserve a Spacesuit: from "The Preservation, Storage, and Display of Spacesuits," Lisa Young & Amanda Young, *Smithsonian National Air & Space Museum*

ACKNOWLEDGMENTS

Deep gratitude to the editors and staff of the following journals in which these poems first appeared (often in earlier versions) for their generous support of this work and of contemporary poetry:

Anti-: "Law of Diminishing Returns" + *Best New Poets/Versal*: "Débridement" + *Black Warrior Review*: "A Daughter Sends the Stenographer a Last Letter from the Moon" + *Bennington Review*: "How to Preserve a Spacesuit" + *Boston Review*, Poetry Contest Winner: "What Would Happen to Your Body in Space Without a Spacesuit," "Landscape in Which I am Obliterated by Light," "Buzz Aldrin's First Words on the Moon as Elegy" (as "Elegy as Yichud Room"), "Microchimera as Lullaby," "Polaroid Ode" + *Colorado Review*: "X-Ray Pastoral" + *Crazyhorse*: "Dilorication Begins at the Silk of a Wrist," "The Way We Sleep" + *The Destroyer*: "Still Life in Réseau Plate" (as "Posing for Francesca Woodman") + *Fairytale Review*: "A Real Spacesuit Is a Little Envelope of Earth Conditions" + *The Foundry*: "A Daughter Drafts a Letter from Earth: Departure" + *Georgetown Review*: "Spacesuit in Early December Woods" (as "Hospital Bed in Early December Woods") + *The Journal*: "*Went Weeping, Little Bones. But Where?,*" "+ [The griever awaits]" (as "Bridal Pyre") + *Memorious*: "Wisteria Strangles the Nearest Body" + *Meridian*: "*All by Myself I Am a Huge Camellia*" + *Mid-American Review*: "Réseau Plate: Interior View with Gemini Constellation" + *West Branch*: "Such & such happens & I hear music," "Ostentatious Still Life with Hospital & Body of"

The writing of this book was made possible by fellowships from the Summer Literary Seminars, University of Utah, and the Lawrence T. and Janet T. Dee Foundation. Special thanks to the Taft-Nicholson Environmental Humanities Center for the time + open skies to both write and finally grieve. May everyone find their Montana.

+

Thank you to my teachers at the University of Utah for supporting all my spacesuits. Especially Kate Coles, Paisley Rekdal, Jackie Osherow, Lance Olsen, Scott Black, and Barry Weller. Thank you also to Gerri Mackey for the sunshine.

Endless affection to my Utah poetry peeps: JP Grasser—there is no grammar of grief without you. Alen Hamza, Jessica Rae Bergamino, Sara Johnson, Paula Mendoza, Jackie Balderama, Ceridwen Hall, & Michelle McFarland—thank you for your light on these poems. Susannah Nevison & David Butcher: your love + flat pennies kept us afloat. Tessa Fontaine: thank you for not being afraid to meet in the grief. To the rest of my Utah cohort in crime: thanks for joining me on the moon.

To Noam Dorr in love + grief + the long haul: there would be no return to earth without you. Thank you for your gentleness + divine desert light, for hours of walking off grief. For holding up every line of our work + never doubting my syntax. For spacesuit-sized maps + notes swapped in class. For every (lucy) moon. For every jar of tea. For seeing + being seen. For knowing: in every life we'll meet.

Infinite thanks to the whole team at Alice James Books—for your eyes and ears and minds. With particular gratitude to Carey Salerno—for seeing this collection as also one of joy. I will carry the wonder and timing of receiving your phone call for a lifetime.

To my brilliant students over the years—thank you for making poetry matter. + To Alice Fulton & Lyrae Van Clief-Stefanon for punctuation as heirloom. + To Justin Boening for your ordering eyes. + To Aleia Nay for watching over our family when we arrived on the moon. + To Zoe Polkadot for keeping us all weird. + To Neal, my Aunts, my extended family, Cat, & Doreen: for your wide-open hearts & Sally stories. + To Joannie & Ronnie for embracing me as family. + To Jenni & Jackie: for remaining the girls of my youth. + To my Poprocks for long walks along the canal in the year after: for being there. + To Nicci for carrying our mother into spring each year. Thank you for every moment & memory of our childhood. + To Z for being unfailingly sure of our decisions, even in galactic darkness. For persistence and the possible future that is always awaiting us—a card pulled from bright air. + To the twin for teaching me how to grieve: forgiveness + To SV & RC, my littlest mittens: for helping create our wild family animal. You make me feel invincible.

+

And to my mother, Sally, in her red coat in every grocery store parking lot: on my best days I send your incredible capacity for love out into the world. I am who I am—every single stitch—because of you.

BOOK BENEFACTORS

Alice James Books wishes to thank the following individual(s) who generously contributed toward the publication of *Little Envelope of Earth Conditions:*

Jeffrey Thomson

For more information about AJB's book benefactor program, contact us via phone or email, or visit alicejamesbooks.org to see a list of forthcoming titles.

RECENT TITLES FROM ALICE JAMES BOOKS

ALICE JAMES BOOKS is committed to publishing books that matter. The press was founded in 1973 in Boston, Massachusetts as a cooperative, wherein authors performed the day-to-day undertakings of the press. This element remains present today, as authors who publish with the press are invited to collaborate closely in the publication process of their work. AJB remains committed to its founders' original feminist mission, while expanding upon the scope to include all voices and poets who might otherwise go unheard. In keeping with its efforts to build equity and increase inclusivity in publishing and the literary arts, AJB seeks out poets whose writing possesses the range, depth, and ability to cultivate empathy in our world and to dynamically push against silence. The press was named for Alice James, sister to William and Henry, whose extraordinary gift for writing went unrecognized during her lifetime.

Designed by Alban Fischer

Printed by McNaughton & Gunn